S.J. LOMAS

In Between

Poems of Midlife

8N PUBLISHING

To every woman struggling to come into her own.
It is your time.

Contents

Preface

Why this book?

I hadn't written poetry since college. It had served its purpose as I pursued my Literature degree and was a challenging, freeing, and enjoyable way to earn credits. My poetry classes were fantastic. So were the professors. But it was something I put aside in favor of work, family, and fiction as the years went on.

When the Covid-19 Pandemic struck, the world screeched to a halt in ways I never thought possible for our busy modern lifestyle. As the days stretched on and on, I found myself losing focus, patience, light, and hope. I wanted to read, but I couldn't concentrate on the words on the page. Books, reading, and writing, my great passions, could not hold my interest anymore and I sadly waited for the day when I could enjoy what I'd once loved so well again.

By January 2021, I was beginning to break through the fog of pandemic life. I discovered that while it was still difficult to read a novel, I could handle reading poetry. More than that, I enjoyed it. I discovered, and rediscovered, the works of Lang Leav, Emily Dickinson, Michael Lawrence, and Derek R. King. I even rediscovered my own poems. I picked up a copy of my own chapbook, *The Blue Muse*, and enjoyed walking through the memories that had inspired each poem. I wondered if I could get back to that place of poetry again.

I pulled out a fresh notebook and opened the cover. With pen in hand,

I wondered if I remembered how to write a poem. Out came "Pandemic Heart." From there, the words and poems began to flow. I found that it was a great balm for me to process the pain and loss I'd endured over the previous two years. I had celebrated my fortieth birthday, determined to embrace the passage into a new decade of life. Within three short months of that milestone birthday, my father's health declined at a dizzying speed and he died. That was not how I expected my fortieth year to begin. After coping with that, the new reality of lockdown life struck. I participated in a drive-through graduation for my daughter after her final year of middle school was cut short by Covid. The claustrophobia of lockdown life. Becoming the manager of my children's virtual learning every day. Shouldering the dependence of my family when I didn't feel any joy or strength myself. Mourning the losses of the life I thought I'd have in the face of a foreign and painful reality. Coping with the journey into middle age during a raging pandemic. There seemed to me, to be a great parallel between moving into middle age and the in between stasis of living in the pandemic. Both provided a viewing point to look before and ahead, reflect, and reassess. I put it all into poetry and felt a great burden lift.

As I found comfort and enjoyment in poetry, I hope someone, perhaps you, will find the same in these pages.

Thank you for reading.

-S.J.

Happy Fortieth

Here's to me
Starting a new decade
A woman who's learned things
Still figuring out others
Not a time of crisis,
a metamorphosis.
Shedding younger woman insecurities
and celebrating what defines me.
I will walk in boldness
Reawaken confidence
Replace preoccupation in pleasing others
with more attention to my needs.
Maybe I'm halfway through.
Could have more ahead
Could have more behind
Time to embrace my terms
Move ahead to dispel regret.
Don't want to reach the end
and find I missed the whole ride.
There's only one me.
Just one dance.
Focus on who I want to be now.
It is my time to shine!

Modern Woman

Maybe she can have it all,
but no one can have all of her.
Splintered pieces go to
every direction,
There's a shard for daughter
A splinter for wife
A heart for each child
A crumb for career
Sometimes there's a star
for her dreams
A glowing mystery
for what she wants to become.
She can have a dance
through everything there is.
She is not all
Of any one thing.
As much a part
as she chooses.

Miracles and Secrets

Two human beings
Began their life journeys
In my body.

It happened to me.
To us.
But it still seems unbelievable.

My favorite thing
Was whenever you moved.
It was our special secret.

At work, I'd hide in a stall
Pull up my shirt
Watch you roll, squirm, and poke.

You did this
With your whole body
Underneath the flesh of mine.

Utterly amazing
And mesmerizing
My precious baby.

We are separate bodies now
I don't know your every move
You are your own secret.

You'll never leave me completely
You left your mark inside
Changed everything about me.

I'll still marvel
At where you came from
A secret in my body, a light into the world.

Mother

Do you ever look at your children
and wonder how they came to be?
The biology of it isn't magic
that's everything in between.
When did they find the sparks
that light them up?
Some things like me.
Some like their dad.
But they are comprised
of their own stuff.
Still a way to go
before they come into their own.
In the end stages of being mostly mine.
Soon to be part of the world
Making a life like I did.

Know Me

If you want to know who I am,
you need to feel my soundtrack
Vibrate with the tones
that touch my core.
Played during moments
they still take me back to.
Elvis, dancing on green carpet
with my daddy.
Watching it rain
from my childhood window.
Wishing so hard for my own Grand Love
Wondering when someone would notice me.
Teenager behind the wheel,
windows open, wind and sun,
heart on the beat
Singing for everyone.
Flying over the ocean,
Walkman in hand.
The playlist of
significant moments.
Opening notes start the movie
of my life in vibrant brilliance again.
An aural embrace
of all my old friends

But the best is not
way far behind.
The music keeps playing.
The minutes continue on.
Both small days
to be forgotten
And bigger ones that shine on.
If you want to know who I am
You need to hear my music.
The chords that make up my heart
The beats that drive my mind.

For Paul

A college professor
can become a lifelong friend.
From Intro to Shakespeare
to poetry critiques in email…
a retirement party…
a graduation celebration…
Christmas cards every year
Respect and camaraderie forever.
Such a big presence
Even from far away.
Always my champion
An enthusiastic fan.
Wish I could send you another message
get another utterly you reply.
No more letters are coming for me.
I have all I'll ever get.
They can't stop me from missing you.
I will never, never, forget.

Who is she?

There's a comfort to everyday life,
but it isn't easy.
Aging doesn't erase the phase before.
Dreams and desires carry over.
Growth, change, perspective,
add more to hold on to.
Daily demands don't cease
The duty of a good wife
A devoted mother
Attentive daughter
Dependable employee…
homemaker…
comfort giver…
Staring in the mirror,
who do you see?
A face becoming less familiar
But you know who's in there.
She changes her focus,
but doesn't fade away.
She's sun on the face
A breeze lifting your hair.
She smells like fresh cut grass in summer,
lilac blossoms in spring,
earthy leaves of autumn,

crisp, snowy, winter air.
She wants to remain a being desired
for who she is inside
Not what she does
Not the role she fulfills.
She never stops being
her own woman
with her own tastes, goals, desires.
Even when her face
Stops matching how she feels.
Take care to remember that
before going out for the day.
It may be hidden
beneath the layers of roles to perform.
The heart will always beat of a woman.

Song About Dying

Mumford & Sons came on the radio
as I drove away from visiting my dad.
"This song is about dying," I thought.
I knew because I'd just seen it all
sitting in my dad's body
as we sat at a table
and my mom fed him soup.
I didn't know how much was left in that body.
It didn't look the same.
He didn't act the same.
The light was fading
I couldn't know when it would go out.
Mom went to fetch something from the kitchen.
Dad reached out and patted my hand.
We smiled at each other.
Father and daughter,
for the last time.
I didn't know it then,
but I cried so hard when that song came on.
The song was about dying
It was going to hit us very soon.
It was coming.
I wasn't ready.
For the rest of my life, I'll never be ready.

Dead Dads Club

I think every daughter goes a little crazy when she loses her dad.
A person who gave you life, now lost their own.
You're still going, but he stopped.
It doesn't make sense.
And I used to believe things so strongly.
But I don't know anymore.

I don't know.

Looking around at the funeral
Reading cards as they come in
I recognize the members of my new club.
I'd extended my sympathy to them at the time,
but I have the understanding now.
Facing the world as a now fatherless daughter.
It's not a thing you know in words.
Just sharp, jagged, feelings.
Not quite confronting mortality
Not clinging to your past
Not defining your new space in the world
That's part, but there's more.
Tears are the right language.
Watching a bird fly past the sun.
Living the same life, passed from him,

for the rest of the days you have.
You don't have to explain.
Daughters in the Dead Dads Club know.

Thursday Night Show

That night at the comedy club
upheld my broken heart.
The jokes landed perfectly
Laughs came easy
And oh, how we laughed!
From deep inside,
Past the yawning chasm of sorrow
Back to the spring of joy that doesn't quite dry.
In the unfathomable territory of loss,
A spark ignited in the eyes of my children.
The new world of improv
Being part of the creative magic of a show
It was good to laugh so hard
And really mean it.
Caught up in the fun of a shared moment
Soaring on the energy of the crowd
Keeping my eyes fixed on my friend in the spotlight,
Shining like a sun, dispelling clouds.
Glad of the invitation to be part of it all
Affirming better days for those whose lives go on.

Isolated but not Alone

The dead may always be with us
but so are the far away
Far from hand
Close to heart
Braided into moments
of everyday life
By a text,
a call,
a video chat,
an email,
a letter
Reaching of one spirit to another.
Maybe one day we'll be together
to kiss, or hug and touch.
For now,
I'll wear your love
as a necklace.
Taking comfort from that.

Firsts

Remember that moment of shining youth?
The headiness of those glorious firsts?
Kisses. Love. Laughter that stretched night to morning.
We were strong then.
Pioneers on the trail of our own lives.
Setting out to stake a claim on our dreams.

It wasn't so long ago.
Not in the blink of a single life.
But long enough in the eyes of the world.

The firsts aren't so gleaming now.
First parent to die. First child to move out.
First one to crack under the pressure.

It's not all lost, but the game has changed.
Not rushing wide-armed to embrace the beginning.
Holding back, trying to make sense before the end.

In Between

To my left, dawn slips, gold over the horizon
Everything the light touches glows.
It's all possibility. Hope. Newness.
Long nights and kisses
Dancing and laughter in crowded halls
Colors as dazzling as the feelings they inspire
I am all power
Dreams
Light.

To my right, sunset dips. Purple down to night.
As it settles, the landscape obscures
It's all murky. Known. Used. Worn.
Short nights and fast days.
Fulfilling routines, expectations, established roles
Colors duller as the experiences are familiar
I am weakening
Reality
Weight.

In between, I straddle the line.
One foot clinging to dawn, the other stepping to night.
Suspended between my beginning and end
Floating for a moment before I fall

Goals, urgency, trials, and comfort
The colors as bright as I care to make them
I am here
Living
Now.

Return Trip

When I turned forty
it was time to go back.
The place that shaped my life,
across the ocean, called too loud to ignore.
Packed up the family
We headed to my past
Sometimes the memory is better than the now
But when my feet stepped down,
My breath came back
The smile spread on my face
Feelings hadn't changed.
I loved as strongly as before.
Some things, still familiar.
Twenty years of change made others new.
Past and present mingling
Creating new delights.
Warm orange stone
Snatches of music from an open theater door
Sunshine bright as my joy
Glinting off the spires of history,
Both ancient and my own.
Written into the same story.
Sparking the flame of new dreams
Reassuring that old ones still live.

A Journey

Once, I took a trip,
Seemingly impossible
certainly impractical
because to not go
would cause regret
for a lifetime.
I wanted to see the place again.
Hoped to recapture that glow
from former youth
But more,
I needed to see you.
Transform fourteen years of words
into a photograph
of an American woman
and an English man
standing on the same patch of earth
arms around each other.
Framed in my room,
those smiling faces remind me
that I did it.
I took an extravagant idea
pursued it
until it became real.
Replacing possible regret down the road

with the shining memory of an afternoon together
After so many years of friendship.

The Memory Box

A box of mementos
jabs my heart with an accusing finger
"You should have savored more."
"You should have said something else."
It's right, of course.
So many mistakes made.
Too many to right now.
All that's left is a box of has been moments.
An air of sweetness
And some regret.

True Love

True love isn't what they show in movies.
It's uglier.
It's hugs with tears, snot, and broken hearts
Blood, vomit, enemas, and operations
Baggy sweatpants and scuffling slippers
A hemorrhoid donut and 3am trips to the ER
The appearance of white hairs and skin spots.

It is not two perfectly gorgeous people
Glistening like diamonds in mind-blowing daily sex marathons
Not constant sunshine smiles
Or laughter and cuddles all night
Flowers, candy, fairy dust and hearts.

Pretty things come easy.
They go easy too.
True love is the people you can surrender to in the mess
And they will not let you go.

Flight of Fancy

Understand, I ebb and flow
In the course of my own vitality.
Talking to you might delight for a month,
then I'm full and content not to speak for a year.
I've learned this about myself. Embraced it.
Every interaction, I give myself.
I don't like to give to many anymore.
Too many demands, for too long.
A noisy world made me feel I must fulfill.
But I don't.
I won't anymore.
There are too few close friends in life
to spend so much on everyone else.
It is okay to replenish my own well.
If thoughts of you become anxiety,
I give myself a pass to let go.
No apologies. I'm not sorry.
It isn't my fault you aren't there for me.
Think I'm rude. Weird. Ill. Busy.
My energy will be spent how I want.
Took too long to realize I don't have to please everyone.
I'm not going back to it now.

Me Now

In my thirties, clear strands of hair started to replace brown.
"Grow old gracefully" is what they say,
But I think they mean dyes, creams, and procedures.
Cosmetics were never much my thing,
but the clear hairs didn't match my youthful face,
or the feeling of who I am
And sometimes highlights, lowlights, and reds are fun.
Somewhere in those colors and dollars,
I wondered what I was becoming underneath.
I grew it all out and found a thin white streak,
visible to me when I brush my hair.
This is me now.
The streak gains new strands every year.
My face gains thin lines too.
The crinkles of my smile don't quite fade away,
but at least they attest to more smiles than frowns.
Call it grace or not,
I will wear this body as it is.
With the scars it bears of battles fought
Lines from the new lives it brought forth.
This is me at forty two.
Showing signs of my journey,
if you know where to look.
Not too altered from what I've been

Changes continue on.
It is not bad to be here.

Memories

Sometimes, memories feel like the realest thing.
I can wrap up in them,
like putting on my favorite sweater.
Close my eyes and feel my way through them again.
Decades fade and I'm that girl again-
walking in darkness, hand in hand,
lips drunk on first kisses.
Running across town at 2am to apologize.
Becoming myself in a foreign city.
Dropping it all on the floor
of a friend who was still alive.
Talking about the Blue Album and life
during a stolen moment in the garage.
A child, gazing at the Christmas Eve sky,
On the way home from the family party.

Traditions end.
Loved ones die.
People fly away,
never to come back.
These things live inside me.
As real as the pen in my hand.
Just a thought away.
Sometimes, I wish so bad to be there again,

But a new song comes on.
I blink and put my sweater of memories
back in the closet until another time.

Pandemic Heart

A year of fragments
Made up from the smashed plans
and dreams
and hope
that a new journey around the sun should bring.
Stopped before the beginning could unfold.
A promise of new days turned to darkness.
Shrieking.
Crying.
A stretch of inertia turned to numbness
Everyday the same.
A number of hours.
Sun up.
Sun down.
Repeat.
Repeat.
Repeat.
Until the life you knew becomes a faint echo in memory.
Impossible to say if it's a true memory or a fiction
shined by the passage of time.
Either way, nothing fits.
Not rhyme and meter.
Not the role I'm meant to fill.
Not the world.

The world…
doesn't fit me like it used to.
Some parts so tight I choke and gasp.
Others so cavernous, I'm swimming
alone in the vastness of the universe
flailing for an anchor to catch hold of.

Days pass in the blinding strobe of time.
Bright Sunday.
Black Monday.
Ad nauseam and sickening
Until, wait…
maybe…
yes!
I hover above time.
I go backwards, tread, and forward at once.
Not linear.
Not cyclical.
All is now.
If it's freeing me or crushing me,
I can't tell.
Scrambling to keep hold of myself,
to remain someone I recognize
But this paused life has strange power.
Stasis strips things down
Grinds off all glitter
and leaves you with grit.
Don't know where I'm going,
but I sure am here.
Here.
HERE!

If the mind is moving forward,
the body stays put.
Ground to a halt.
Locked in a staring contest with how I thought life would be.
Guess I blinked.
Now I'm here in the void with the rest of you.
Some of us are floating
Riding the ripples together.
Some are clomping along, defiant,
just daring to be caught.

Not sure how much longer I will last.
Send help.

Time Flies

Pandemics are events for the history books
sidenotes to ancestral life
Not something that occurs in my planner
And then stalls out my days.
March 13, 2020 - the last day my kids set foot in school
January 23, 2021 - virtual school fatigue beats us all
Nearly a year now. What can we show?
Tedious days passing one at a time
Birthdays, anniversaries, cancelled trips, holidays.
Is something supposed to be special today?
Time is not linear anymore.
Yesterday is tomorrow is last month
Is an hour from now, is today.
I cooked meat and didn't add onion.
Basic thing I've done countless times.
My mind didn't register at all.
When all your days, events, and people are missing,
how can you notice an onion?
Tired of getting through it
Unsure if I'm really fine or just pretending
Days are long and short together.
Treading the moments of our lives.

Don't Remember

No one living this
Will want to think of it again.
Memories of waking up,
Plodding through day until night
Are almost as numbing
as doing it.
I don't write to preserve these moments
I write to move through them.
Preserve a sense of purpose
Create value in stagnant times.
Mind transcends the bindings of body
Moves onward, beyond, while bones sit.
Static buzzes around and through each day,
The hum of hope pulses while creating.

Small Things

Life is very small now
Stifling.
Saint Therese, the Little Flower,
lived a "little way"
Did "small things with great love."
I do small things with a great void.
Thumbing the moments of my life,
They flash by, float away. Forever gone.
My life is ticking.
I don't notice it moving.
Days used to be filled
with people, places, things to do.
I see three faces every day.
Their lives are ticking too.
Small pleasures for small lives.
That's what we have now.
Not bad.
Different.
A warm shower.
Animal tracks in snow.
The moonrise.
Dazzling sunsets.
Perfectly brewed tea.
Laughing again after crying.

Our days are much smaller than they used to be.
But they're still ours.

Winter Sunshine

Sunshine smashes into the house
The only visitor we've seen in months.
Eyes drawn to the sight
I discover the snow sparkling like celestial diamonds.
The spell so intoxicating,
Grabbing coat and gloves, I dash outside
Sun so dazzling in a winter blue sky.
My eyes squint and water
Air so cold I gasp
My nose runs down my face like a child's
This is real.
This is now.
Trapped as I am,
I'm still in the world
Sun and air.
Cold and light
touch my body.
A wild but welcome friend.
The rough embrace awakens me again
Grounded in life for another day.

Teenager

Funny how it seems so recently I was a teen.
Flexing new wings. Looking for boys. Driving with friends.
Now it's my daughter's turn
And my own teen dreams feel worlds away.
Instead of freshman year, a new beginning,
She faces a progression of ends.
Lockdown at home. Virtual life.
No laughter with friends. No parties. No dances. No boys.
It's a limited time adventure as it is.
A computer screen of assignments holds no magic moments.
It's a hard time to be trapped in this limbo.
She should be starting to fly.
I was beginning to know how to soar.
Here we are, trying to be more while stuck in less.
Both our worlds should be expanding in new ways.
The struggle of mom and daughter
More tense for all the frustration.
No where to get away.
No new space to grow into.
I don't remember how hard it was.
For her, it is much harder.
Hold on my limbo teenager
Your time isn't lost, just delayed.
Your cramped wings will unfurl

I'll watch you fly higher than you dream possible.

Enough

I don't understand some people
What motivates them?
The things they find important
How they must spend time
The pandemic gift, for me,
is gratitude and the grace of enough
I haven't purchased clothing in a year.
My closet still overflows.
I don't know the last time I sat in a restaurant.
I eat generous meals everyday.
The morning rush is replaced with morning calm.
We get up when we're ready, when our own bodies say.
I don't miss a lot of what the world said was life.
Rushing, buying, going, being seen.
It's a survival mode, yes.
Snow falls outside my window
I'll stay in my home for another day
but I stay with the family I created.
The husband I chose.
The daughter and son we made.
What a luxury it would have seemed,
to pause the world and be together.
It took a crisis, but some things we lost are good.
We are healthy.

We are loved.
We have enough.

Monday Morning

The sun shining through a bottle of cleaner next to my tub
is no less exquisite
than the way light plays across mountain crags in Montana
because this bottle
and a ray of sun
are my reality right now
and beauty is found anywhere

About the Author

S.J. Lomas is one of a few pen names for this multi-faceted author. Writing as S.J. she flirts with darker themes and dives into emotion. This is her second collection of poetry. She never knows exactly what she'll feel like writing next. Keep up with her on social media to stay aware of new projects.

You can connect with me on:
- http://www.sjlomas.com
- https://twitter.com/AlanaOxford

Also by S.J. Lomas

S.J. has written heartfelt poetry, supernatural short stories, and a YA duology. She also writes as Alana Oxford - humorous women's fiction, romcoms, and sweet contemporary romance.

The Blue Muse

A collection of poetry covering themes of love, music, family, friendship, and nation.

Winter Chills

In the spirit of seasonal ghost stories, this wintry collection will send a tingle down your spine, but may also warm your heart.

Six short stories range from waiting for a mysterious midnight train, attending a party with an unexpected guest, a life-changing reunion for a miserable family, receiving a holiday greeting unlike any other, a visit from an unusual group of carolers, and a journey through a blizzard with a twist.

Grab a blanket, your favorite hot drink, and settle in for some Winter Chills.

Stories included:
   By D.B. Carter: Departures and Arrivals,
   The Christmas Card
By Derek R. King: Defying Convention
By S.J. Lomas: The Holiday Party,
   The Carolers
By Natalie Reeves-Billing: Go With the Wind

Dream Girl

From the day Gabriel starts working with Christine at the library, he turns her life upside-down with sizzling chemistry, bizarre stories, and incredible dreams. Dreams so vivid they feel like real life.

Christine's friends think she's falling for Gabriel fast but they don't know about the secret life Gabriel and Christine are living at night. Who would believe her if she told? As the dreams become more dangerous, it's clear they're being orchestrated by someone. But who? And more importantly, why?

As Christine struggles to help Gabriel unravel the secrets of the dreamworld, she risks her closest friendships, her college plans, and maybe even her life.

Dream Frequency

Gabriel and Christine are prepped and ready for entrance into a top secret government agency. It should be a cinch for Gabriel to ace his final test while Christine prepares to enter training and say goodbye to her friends.

But on the eve of Gabriel's test, at a time when Christine's friends need her most, a disturbing development threatens everything. An anonymous enemy sets them in a race against time to rid the agency of deep seated corruption and sabotage before the unthinkable happens. Who can they trust?

To save themselves and everyone who matters to them, they must choose their allegiances wisely, and risk it all, friends, future, their very lives. Will they succeed or die trying?

This thrilling conclusion to Dream Girl can also be read on its own as a complete novel.

Blue Skies

Life isn't always a walk in the park, but when Patrice takes her Pomeranians to the park after a rough day at the office, fate steps in. An unlikely hero comes to the rescue when one of her dogs gets loose. Short, pale, and kind of cute, Seth doesn't have a lot of confidence with the ladies, but he hits it off with Patrice.

But some things might be too good to be true. While Patrice wonders if Seth could possibly be "the one", fate steps in again with a horrible twist. Will it be a deal breaker or just a storm before bright blue skies?